A special thank-you for

You have touched my life.
Thank you for being there.

With gratitude,

Date

---

thank you

for being there

a collection of poems,
prayers, stories, quotes, and
scriptures to say thank you

HOWARD
PUBLISHING CO.

thank
you

Your presence

brought light to

my darkest days.

Dear _____,

Our world is a challenging place. Sometimes it's far more complicated than we can deal with alone. We all have times when things pile up or fall apart—when weariness presses in upon our spirits, and we feel burdened and alone. We long to see some light at the end of the tunnel and hope someone will come to lend a hand.

I am so thankful that you dared to be the friend I needed during such a time. Demanding nothing in return, you cared enough to share my distress and shoulder my load.

It's comforting to know that you can be counted on to be there in difficult times. You've made a difference in my life. I can never thank you enough.

I hope the words of this little book will return a blessing to you for the kindness you've shown. Thank you for being there.

Sincerely,

Brilliance,
genius,
competence—
all are subservient
to the quality
of faithfulness.

WALLACE FRIDY

Grace and Glory

The darkness was closing in on Grace even though it was broad daylight. She walked wearily out of the doctor's office where she had just been diagnosed with severe depression. It was no wonder after all she'd been through.

For as long as Grace could remember, she had wanted a large, church wedding. She'd begun planning for it in third grade. Her dream wedding included a strapless, Cinderella-style gown with a chapel-length veil, a single strand of pearls, white satin ballet slippers, a generous bouquet of white roses, six stunning bridesmaids dressed in lavender and lace, a wide gold wedding band sporting a simple one-carat diamond solitaire, a silver-haired minister, and flowers—flowers everywhere.

In spite of all the dreaming, Grace's *actual* wedding took place in the courthouse downtown with a balding justice of the peace and two witnesses from the office of the county clerk. She had worn a lime-green, tie-dyed T-shirt and faded blue jeans that were too tight across her tummy, since she was four months pregnant. Her ring had been purchased at a discount store near the mall. It was silver-plated. And there were no flowers—no flowers anywhere.

When Grace phoned her mom the next morning to tell her that she was married, she'd heard a gasp, a sob, a click, and a dial tone.

Grace had been so predictable, so dependable, until she met Chuck during her sophomore year. Chuck the Charmer, everyone called him. She had been attending college on an academic scholarship. Chuck was just hanging out around campus, hitting on girls. He had trouble holding down a job and lacked any real ambition. Ever since he entered the picture, things had deteriorated.

Grace miscarried two weeks after the wedding. Chuck never even showed up at the hospital.

When Grace phoned her mom the morning after to tell

her that she'd been pregnant and lost the baby, she heard another gasp, another sob, another click, and another dial tone.

Grace filed for divorce one year later.

Her mom cried and hung up again when Grace called to announce that she was divorced.

At the age of twenty-one, Grace felt she had lived a lifetime of heartache. It seemed that for all of her good intentions, nothing had gone as she had planned. She had lost her baby, failed at marriage, alienated her parents, dropped out of college, and accumulated a mountain of debt in the process. It would take a couple of years to pay things off—to get back on her feet—then she hoped to resume her education. Her parents had withdrawn their financial support completely.

That day, on the verge of giving up, Grace took a detour by the library. Her library card was about to expire, and she wanted to renew it. That card was the last shred of evidence that she had once been headed somewhere and her last hope that she might again. Her face flushed when the library clerk commented, "Grace Mallett, huh? Are you sure you want to do this?

Renewing your card will cost five dollars, and you haven't used yours in over two years."

"I guess inflation has hit the library industry pretty hard, huh?" Grace shot back to deflect her embarrassment. She noticed that an older woman seemed to be listening in on their conversation.

Grace spent the next two hours poring over old, familiar classics, carefully selecting those she would check out. At one point, she spontaneously broke down and sobbed with remorse over the condition of her life. Only two short years ago she had been a regular at this library, shuffling and reshuffling books, thriving on the pursuit of her academic dreams. Now she wasn't even sure she wanted to go on living. Grace swallowed a last lump that felt lodged in her throat as she approached the counter for the second time.

"Are you a student?" the same clerk inquired this time as Grace handed her the pile of books.

"Not at the moment," Grace answered, blushing again. "I'm taking some time off. But what does that have to do with any-thing?"

Washington acepta la espada de Cornwallis.

Washington sabía que los barcos franceses iban camino a Yorktown. Podían bloquear las provisiones y las tropas que Cornwallis esperaba. También podían impedir que los británicos apostados en Yorktown se fueran por mar una vez que empezara

Con parte de enfermo

Cornwallis no se rindió ante Washington en persona. Dijo que se sentía muy enfermo para ir. En cambio, envió a su segundo al mando para ofrecer a Washington su espada y rendirse.

la lucha. Pero Washington necesitaba tropas en tierra. Sus hombres y los soldados franceses estaban en Rhode Island. Eso era a 500 millas de distancia. ¿Podrían llegar caminando a tiempo para la batalla? ¡Sí, podrían!

Los soldados estadounidenses y franceses cavaron trincheras e instalaron sus cañones en las afueras de Yorktown. ¡Y después atacaron! Cuando los británicos se despertaron esa mañana, estaban rodeados. ¡Quedaron atrapados! El combate duró tres semanas. Después, Cornwallis se rindió. El 19 de octubre de 1781, todo había terminado. Los británicos no pudieron recuperarse después de esa batalla. Estados Unidos se preparó para ganar la guerra. En 1783, Estados Unidos de América se convirtió oficialmente en una nación independiente.

"These are pretty heavy-duty volumes," the young woman said as she scanned the books. "I just want to make sure you really want five of them. Being so near the university, we have a great demand for this kind of literature."

"I'll return them on time," Grace answered with an edge in her voice. She filed her new library card in her wallet and slid the books off the counter and into her arms indignantly.

"I'm looking for Ernest Hemingway's *For Whom the Bell Tolls*," a thin, female voice said to the clerk as Grace turned to leave. "You had two copies the day before yesterday, and now there are none." It was the old woman Grace had noticed earlier. She looked distressed.

"Sorry, Grandma," the clerk shot back, "the last volume is just leaving the building. You should have grabbed one while you had the chance."

Grace was appalled! Who did the clerk think she was to speak to an elderly woman in that tone of voice? *And calling her Grandma!*

"Pardon me," Grace said loudly to the clerk so the elderly woman would hear, "I just checked out the last copy of *For*

Whom the Bell Tolls, but I've had a change of heart. I really wanted Tolstoy's *Anna Karenina.* Could you please make the exchange for me?"

Once outside, Grace plopped down on a park bench in the shade of a massive oak tree. Its sprawling branches cast a deep, cool shade. Grace found relief in the moment. She opened *Anna Karenina.*

"Thank you...Grace, isn't it?" It was the same sweet voice from inside the library. "For letting Mr. Hemingway accompany me this afternoon. This was my Davy's favorite book," she explained. "I go to his grave and read a section of it to him every year on the anniversary of his death. We met at a library, you see. Otherwise I would just buy a copy. By the way, my name is Gloria. My friends call me Grandma Glory," she grinned.

"How did you know my name?" Grace was curious.

"The clerk said it," she answered. "Grace Mallett. I had a daughter named Grace. We called her Gracie."

"Oh," Grace said with interest, "and who was Davy?"

"My husband." She smiled, remembering things past. "He died sixteen years ago."

"How sad," Grace said compassionately. "I'm so sorry."

"Oh, it's OK. He couldn't wait to see Gracie," she continued. "Gracie died of leukemia when she was only seven. She loved to read, just like you."

"Do you have any other children?" Grace was growing concerned about the woman.

"No." She looked away for a brief moment, her eyes glistening. Turning slowly, she sat carefully, painfully on the bench beside Grace. "But Gracie filled our hearts and lives completely. We were so glad we had her for as long as we did."

A long silence followed. Grace thought the conversation was over and went back to her reading.

"I don't mean to be nosey, Grace," the woman suddenly spoke, "but I overheard you say your education is on hold. May I ask why?"

Grace lowered the book again. She looked at the woman sitting with her hands folded neatly on top of Hemingway's classic. Her eyes searched Grace's with compassion.

"I was in a bad marriage for just over a year, and I have some things to straighten out, that's all." Grace blushed with humiliation again. "I'm just a little strapped financially right now."

"I was troubled to see you crying inside," Grandma Glory continued.

It must have been her genuine concern that made Grace open up. The two sat for hours as Grace spilled her heartache into the kind woman's lap. And Grace listened in turn as the woman shared her story of love and loss.

Their hearts connected across several generations.

Finally the woman said, "It's getting late, and I need to be going. Could I have your address? I'll be finished with Mr. Hemingway day after tomorrow, and I'd like to send him back to you. Could you possibly return him to the library for me?"

"I'd be glad to," Grace responded. She tore her address from a deposit slip and pressed it into the woman's hand. "Thanks so much for listening. I suppose I needed a friend."

"I suppose we all do, dear." Grandma Glory smiled knowingly and nodded good-bye.

Two days later, Grace received a small box in the mail. The phone began ringing, and she fumbled to open the package quickly. Inside was Hemingway. Smiling, Grace picked up the phone.

"Grace Mallett?" the voice said on the other end of the line.

"Yes?" Grace answered, distracted. A note was tucked into the pages of the book.

"This is Jenny with the registrar's office at the university," the voice continued. I'm calling to inform you that you have a tuition credit of $25,000. It may be applied to your books and supplies, as well. Your benefactor has commissioned me to ask whether you'll be enrolling this semester?"

"What in the world?" Grace was astounded. "There must be some mistake..."

"Grace Mallett of 1214 Clarence Street?" the voice verified.

"That's me." Grace was confused.

"A two-year cafeteria credit and a parking pass have also been purchased on your behalf," Jenny said. "Just drop by our office tomorrow to register."

Finishing the conversation, Grace opened the note. It read simply: *"Dear Grace, thank you for giving up Hemingway for us. It will be the last time I'll read it to Davy. The bell now tolls for me. Waste no more time on tears, my friend. Get on with your education and with living. And Grace, thank God, for Glory belongs to Him."*

During the next two years, as Grace finished her degree, she visited the library many times, always hoping to see Grandma Glory. She never found the kind woman to thank her. But every night, Grace gets down on her knees and thanks God for His Glory.

Grace and Glory

thank
you

Thank you for

bringing laughter

when my world

was silent.

a blessing
for you

May every act of tenderness and kindness that you've shown

Be rewarded by heaven's gracious love.

May every encouragement and merciful deed you've done

Be returned to you—a gift from above.

for being there

for being there

For each time you've served and bent to bear a load.

For the generous way you share your life, your peace.

I pray blessings multiply for you a hundredfold,

The abundance of eternal love increased.

Psalm
23:4
NIV

EVEN THOUGH
I WALK
THROUGH
THE VALLEY
OF THE SHADOW
OF DEATH,
I WILL
FEAR NO EVIL,
FOR YOU ARE
WITH ME.

thank
you

Your faithfulness

has been a

healing balm

for my soul.

To a Friend

You entered my life in a casual way,
    And saw at a glance what I needed;
There were others who passed me or met me each day,
    But never a one of them heeded.
Perhaps you were thinking of other folks more,
    Or chance simply seemed to decree it;
I know there were many such chances before,
    But the others—well, they didn't see it.
You said just the thing that I wished you would say,
    And you made me believe that you meant it;
I held up my head in the old gallant way,
    And resolved you should never repent it.
There are times when encouragement means such a lot,
    And a word is enough to convey it;

There were others who could have, as easy as not—
 But, just the same, they didn't say it.
There may have been someone who could have done more
 To help me along, though I doubt it;
What I needed was cheering, and always before
 They had let me plod onward without it.
You helped to refashion the dream of my heart,
 And made me turn eagerly to it;
There were others who might have (I question that part)—
 But, after all, they didn't do it!

—Grace Stricker Dawson

We are not
primarily put on
this earth
to see through
one another,
but to see
one another
through.

PETER DEVRIES

Down, but Not Out

The warm cookies cooling on the counter gave the kitchen a cozy appearance and delicious aroma.

Lily's bed was neatly made up; three ruffled pillows added a finishing touch. Everything seemed just as it should be, and it was...mostly...except for Lily herself.

Lily never should have been home to make those cookies or oversee the cleaning. She should have been explaining her great new advertising campaign. That would have been the proper place for Lily, not sitting in a wheelchair directing Nona to do work she once could do easily herself.

"Nona, you can go now. Everything looks great. Thanks again for your help," Lily said with affection and gratitude.

"I'll see you tomorrow, Lily," Nona called as she left.

Through the window Lily watched Nona's old but immaculately maintained car disappear down the street, then turned her eyes the other direction to see if her best friend, Anna, was coming. A stay-at-home mom, Anna lived only three blocks away. She had promised to come by this morning at ten o'clock to show Lily the kids' new school pictures.

With no children of her own, Lily had always lived her "family life" through Anna; and Anna, with no career, had lived her "career life" through Lily. Occasionally, each had wished she could trade places with the other.

But Lily knew no one would want to trade places with her now—not since that horrible night a year ago. Anna had picked up Lily for a girls' night out: away from kids, jobs, and responsibilities. As the harried mother of three teenagers, Anna felt the girls' night out was truly essential. What Lily loved was having her friend all to herself, like in the old days.

Lily had forgotten the details of the accident due to her head injury, but she'd heard the story many times. Anna, the driver, wore her seat belt; Lily did not. Another car came out of nowhere and crossed the median. On impact, Lily was thrown twenty-five feet. Her neck was broken. Anna explained later that Lily had been so focused on telling about two coworkers' possible romance, she'd simply forgotten to buckle up. Now Lily was reminded daily of how costly "simply forgetting" could be.

It could have been worse, Lily knew. She had recovered from her head injuries, and she still could use her arms. She would return to work once she mastered a few more skills, but for now she would wait. She had no choice.

Lily looked at her watch. Anna was late.

Anna's never late, she thought with a touch of concern.

She recalled the many times she had ridden to school with Anna. For an instant she was a teenager again. She was almost ready for school, and she could hear Anna's car horn blaring impatiently. She smiled at the memory.

No, Anna is never late.

She wheeled herself to the telephone. A knot began forming in her stomach as she dialed Anna's number.

No one answered the phone's persistent ringing. Lily wheeled herself back to the front room to look out the window again. Thirty more minutes went by as Lily's panic grew. She couldn't drive, she couldn't run—she couldn't even wheel herself three blocks.

"OK, God, help me figure this one out. I'm stuck!" she pleaded for wisdom.

Then it came to her. *Call Nona.* She drew a deep breath, feeling instant relief. She knew how dependable Nona was; she could always count on her.

"Nona, can you come back?" Lily asked apologetically but urgently when Nona answered the phone. "Something must have happened to Anna. She's nearly an hour overdue and doesn't answer her phone."

"Oh!" Nona replied. "I'll go right over and check on her."

"No, I have to go with you. Please come and get me," Lily insisted.

"I'll be right there," Nona promised.

Lily could hardly contain herself. Her concern for her friend seemed almost strong enough to make her get up and walk. Almost. Frustrated again at her limitations, she waited impatiently for help.

Nona arrived and quickly pushed Lily's wheelchair down the ramp from the front porch to the driveway. She helped Lily into the passenger seat. Lily immediately fastened her seatbelt.

After the wheelchair had been stowed in the trunk, they headed toward Anna's house.

They arrived in record time. Anna's car was parked in the driveway, but the front door was locked. No one answered the doorbell's repeated summons. Increasingly alarmed, Lily told Nona where to find the spare key, under an outdoor flowerpot.

Lily was right behind Nona, ready to push her way into the room as soon as the door was opened. She wheeled quickly through the house, calling urgently for Anna. There was no answer, no sign of her friend. Even Anna's purse was missing from the place she kept it when she was at home.

Then she heard it—a faint cry from the backyard. Lily didn't wait for Nona to push her. She wheeled around so quickly she nearly turned herself over as she hurried to the back door and opened it. Nona raced to catch up and ease Lily down the small step so she wouldn't fall out of the chair onto the patio.

There was Anna, lying in the backyard with roses scattered around her head, the contents of her purse spilled just out of reach. Her pale, sweating face grimaced in obvious pain.

"Thank God, you're here," Anna wept in relief. "My ankle hurts so much. I think it's broken."

"What happened?" Lily asked in horror as Nona knelt beside Anna and gently probed the swollen ankle.

"I picked some roses to bring you," Anna explained with a touch of embarrassment. "But I stepped in a hole and came down hard. I can't stand up. I yelled for help, but no one heard me. My cell phone's dead. You were my only hope. I kept thinking, *Lily knows I'm never late.* I just knew you'd be here—wheelchair and all."

"We've always been there for each other," Lily said solemnly. "Today you needed me. Of course I'd be here.

"And now, my faithful friend," Lily announced with exaggerated pomp, "with the help of another faithful friend," she nodded at Nona, "it's time to 'be there' for each other at the hospital."

Nona smiled appreciatively at Lily's recognition, and even Anna managed a pained laugh. "From the feel of this ankle, you just might have to teach me how to steer my own wheelchair for a few days," she joked.

"Or maybe this time *I'll* give *you* a ride," Lily shot back, patting her lap invitingly.

"I'll be there!" Anna laughed.

"Yes," Lily said gratefully. "I know you always will be."

thank
you

With you

in my life,

I never

feel alone.

Philemon
1:4
NIV

I ALWAYS
THANK MY
GOD AS I
REMEMBER
YOU IN MY
PRAYERS.

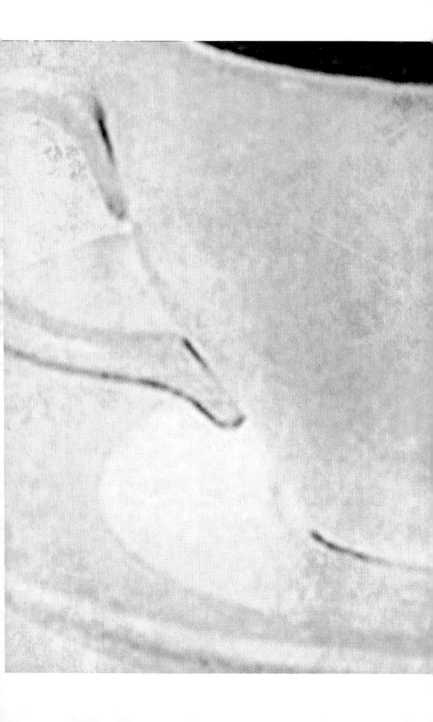

The Human Touch

'Tis the human touch in this world that counts,
    The touch of your hand and mine,
Which means far more to the fainting heart
    Than shelter and bread and wine;
For shelter is gone when the night is o'er,
    And bread lasts only a day,
But the touch of the hand and the sound of the voice
    Sing on in the soul alway.

—Spencer Michael Free

thank you

Like a soft and

steady rain, your

constancy has

refreshed my

weary heart.

Dear Heavenly Father,

How can I thank You for the presence of this special person in my life? The blessing she has been to me during this trying time is beyond expression. Her willingness to be there when I needed a friend reflects Your faithfulness.

She reminds me of You—running to me when I'm in need, lifting me up when I'm down, encouraging me when I feel weak. And though it's impossible to adequately express the depth of my feelings, I know You understand.

So, Lord, I pray that You will bless her as richly as she deserves. Wrap her heart in a tender, heavenly hug, and help her to know that she's valued. And, Father, please help me to learn from her example. Grant me the same gift of insight, that I might be there for her as she has been for me.

Amen.

Those who
bring sunshine to
the lives of others
cannot keep it
from themselves.

JAMES BARRIE